WRITING SENTENCES

How to Write Sentences People Love to Read!

WRITING SENTENCES

How to Write Sentences People Love to Read!

Published by
Heron Books, Inc.
20950 SW Rock Creek Road
Sheridan, OR 97378

heronbooks.com

Fifth Edition © 1976, 2021 Heron Books
All Rights Reserved

ISBN: 978-0-89-739144-3

Any unauthorized copying, translation, duplication or distribution, in whole or in part, by any means, including electronic copying, storage or transmission, is a violation of applicable laws.

The Heron Books name and the heron bird symbol are registered trademarks of Delphi Schools, Inc.

Printed in the USA

10 June 2021

At Heron Books, we think learning should be engaging and fun. It should be hands-on and allow students to move at their own pace.

To facilitate this, we have created a learning guide that will help any student progress through this book, chapter by chapter, with confidence and interest.

Get learning guides at
heronbooks.com/learningguides.

For a final exam, email
teacherresources@heronbooks.com

We would love to hear from you!
Email us at *feedback@heronbooks.com.*

In This Book

1 LET'S GET STARTED! 1
    Putting Words Together 1

2 WHAT IS A SENTENCE? 5

3 WHAT IS A NOUN? 7
    Easy Nouns 8
    Trickier Nouns 10

4 WHAT IS A VERB? 15
    Verbs That Show Action 15
    A Game to Play with Action Verbs 18
    A Game to Play with Nouns and Action Verbs 19
    Verbs That Show Being 20
    Verbs Can Work Together 23

5 NOUN OR VERB? 29

6 PAST, PRESENT OR FUTURE? 33
    Present Tense 35
    Future Tense 35
    Past Tense 36

7 FUNNY VERBS 37
Present Tense 37
Past Tense 40
Future Tense 43

8 ING? 45

9 WORDS THAT DESCRIBE 49

10 WHAT IS AN ADJECTIVE? 51

11 WHAT IS AN ADVERB? 55
Adverbs with Verbs 56
Adverbs with Adjectives 59
Adverbs with Other Adverbs 61

12 A, AN AND THE 63

13 WOW, LOOK WHAT YOU KNOW! 69

14 HOW TO STOP A SENTENCE 73

15 HOW TO PAUSE A SENTENCE 77

16 HOW TO START SENTENCES AND NAMES 79
Starting a Sentence 79
Naming People and Things 80
Days of the Week 80
Names of the Months 80
But Not the Seasons 81

17 HOW TO WRITE A GREAT SENTENCE 83
Parts of a Sentence 83
Sentences That Tell 87
Sentences That Ask 88
Too Short? 89
Too Long? 90
Sentences People Love to Read 90

18 THE MAGIC SECRET 93

Let's Get Started!

PUTTING WORDS TOGETHER

We use words to talk about different things.

bike *skateboard*

But the order you put the words in can make a big difference. Let's say two different things using these words:

a
dog
girl
hair
has
long
the
with

LET'S GET STARTED!

The girl with long hair has a dog.   *The girl has a dog with long hair.*

They are the same words but in different order. They mean very different things, don't they?

If you don't put words together right, people get confused.

LET'S GET STARTED!

When you put words together right, people understand you.

Using words correctly and putting them together in the right order is called **grammar.**

Even if you've never heard the word *grammar* before, you actually already know a lot about grammar! You've been talking to people for a long time so you usually know the right way to use words so that people understand you. That's grammar!

Maybe when you were just a baby, you said, "Apple mine." Now you would probably say, "Hey, that apple's mine!"

Maybe when you were a little older, you said, "Mommy, I runned to the store!" Now you would say, "Hey, Mom, I just ran to the store."

You've learned grammar by listening to people who use words correctly and by talking a lot and wanting to make sure people understand you.

LET'S GET STARTED!

You've also learned a lot about grammar by reading books by people who are experts at using words correctly to tell a great story.

And you've been writing for a while too, so you've been learning how to make sure people understand *your* stories or other things you've written about.

Look at this:

Joe and Chad is talk and play together.

Sounds funny, right? That's because the grammar isn't right.

Joe and Chad are talking and playing together.

That sounds better. That's correct grammar.

Part of grammar is understanding what *sentences* are and how they work, and that's what this book is all about:

Writing sentences people love to read!

If you're not sure what a sentence is, don't worry. That's what this book is all about!

What Is a Sentence? 2

Understanding sentences is the first thing to know about putting words together right. And the first thing to know about sentences is this:

A **sentence** is a group of words that tells a whole idea. It's a group of words that makes sense when you say them.

Take a look at this example:

In the afternoon

That's not really a whole idea, it's only part of an idea. And it doesn't make sense without more words.

Here's one way to make it a sentence:

In the afternoon we will go swimming.

Now it tells a whole idea and it makes sense.

Here's another example:

to become a scientist

Hm. That doesn't really make sense without more words, does it? Let's add some words so it sounds like a whole idea and makes sense:

WHAT IS A SENTENCE?

Miguel plans to become a scientist.

Ah, that's much better isn't it? It says a whole idea. And it makes sense. That's because it's a sentence!

But that's just the beginning of understanding sentences. Want to learn more? Just turn the page.

What Is a Noun?

3

One part of every sentence is something called a *noun*.

A **noun** is a word that names a person, place or thing.

Bill *store*

WHAT IS A NOUN?

EASY NOUNS

Most nouns are pretty easy to figure out. Those are the nouns that name persons, places or things that you can see, touch, smell, taste or hear.

cactus

grapes

onion

bell

girl

WHAT IS A NOUN?

Look around you right now and name some things you see, like maybe *table*, *chair* or *book*. Go ahead, look around.

Did you do that?

The words that name those things are nouns.

For example, the word used to describe the object below is *bicycle.*

Nouns are *words* that name persons, places or things.

This is a bicycle. The bicycle itself is not a noun, but the word *bicycle* is a noun.

Now close your eyes and see if you can smell something. Maybe you can smell the soap you used to wash your hands. Maybe you can smell food being prepared in another room. If you put a crayon, marker or eraser close to your nose, you can probably smell them.

Those words are all nouns—*soap, food, crayon, marker* and *eraser.* Why? They are nouns because a noun is a word that names a person, place or thing. The easiest nouns are the ones you can see, smell, hear, touch or taste.

Let's try one more. Close your eyes and listen. Maybe you can hear your friend or a car or a bird. What are the nouns?

If you said the words *friend* or *car* or *bird* or whatever words name the things you heard, that's right. Those words are all nouns.

That's pretty easy, isn't it? You can probably think of many nouns.

WHAT IS A NOUN?

TRICKIER NOUNS

Nouns can also name things that you cannot see, touch, smell, taste or hear. These can be a little trickier to spot.

Did you ever think about how there could be things you can't see, touch, smell, taste or hear? Here are some examples:

idea
time
courage
happiness
peace

An *idea* is a thing, and *time* is a thing, but you can't exactly see them or smell them or touch them or taste them or hear them. But they are still things. It's the same with *happiness, peace* and *courage*.

When you write and talk, most of the nouns you use are the easy ones. But you also use words like *happiness* and *courage* because those things are part of your life. The words used to name those things are nouns also. They're just a little trickier, don't you think?

Here are a few more examples:

The storm made Jens shiver with fear.

WHAT IS A NOUN?

You can see a storm and you could see a person whose names is Jens. (Remember a noun names a person, place or thing. Jens is a person. A storm is a thing.) Those are easy nouns to spot.

How about fear? You can't see fear, or taste it, or smell it, or touch it, or hear it. But it's still a thing.

The words *storm, Jens* and *fear* are all nouns in that sentence.

Her face was bright with joy.

The word *face* is an easy noun to spot. You can touch your face! You can't really touch *joy,* but the word *joy* is also a noun because it names a thing.

Miguel had a confusion.

WHAT IS A NOUN?

The word *Miguel* is an easy noun to spot because you could touch or see Miguel. But the word *confusion* is a trickier noun. You can't touch a confusion, but it is a thing. So the word *confusion* is a noun.

But what about places? We didn't give any examples of places. Can you think of some places?

Here are some examples of nouns that name places:

Tokyo
airport
village
Clear Lake
Mexico

The important thing is that all nouns are

words that name a person, place or thing.

Some nouns are easy to see, some are trickier. But if they name a person, place or thing, they are nouns.

Here's a picture with lots of nouns. All but one of them are the easier kind to spot. Can you spot the trickier one? It's a thing, but not a thing you can touch, taste, hear, smell or see.

WHAT IS A NOUN?

Nouns are important parts of all sentences.

But sentences have another important part. To write sentences that make sense, you need more than nouns. The next chapter is about another important part of sentences.

What Is a Verb?

4

A **verb** is a word that tells what a person or thing does or the way it is.

VERBS THAT SHOW ACTION

These verbs show what someone or something is *doing*.

I run every day.

The horse gallops.

These verbs that show action are called **action verbs**.

Words like *talk, sing, dance, laugh, cry, play, write, read* and *shout* are all action verbs. Can you think of some more?

15

WHAT IS A VERB?

Here are some more examples:

She jumps fast.   *Marcella waves "hello!"*

Sometimes the action is something you can't exactly see because the action is in your mind. Here are some examples of action verbs showing things happening in a person's mind.

The woman dreams.   *Rupert thinks a lot.*

WHAT IS A VERB?

Sometimes the action isn't about something moving, but we still call it an action verb. Here are some examples:

My sister <u>owns</u> a car.

I <u>love</u> blueberries!

There are many, many verbs that show action. Can you think of some more? Can you think of 10 more? Can you think of 20?

If you took some time, you could probably think of more than a hundred verbs that show action. (Hint: If you look in a dictionary that says when words are nouns or verbs, you will find *thousands* of action verbs!)

WHAT IS A VERB?

A GAME TO PLAY WITH ACTION VERBS

Here's something fun to do with action verbs.

Make a sentence and then change the verb over and over to make different sentences. Here are some examples:

Susie <u>walks</u> across the room.

Susie <u>crawls</u> across the room.

Susie <u>runs</u> across the room.

Susie <u>skips</u> across the room.

Susie <u>slides</u> across the room.

Susie <u>tumbles</u> across the room.

Susie <u>hops</u> across the room.

Susie <u>dances</u> across the room.

Susie <u>rushes</u> across the room.

Susie <u>shouts</u> across the room.

This game is a great way to get really good with action verbs!

WHAT IS A VERB?

A GAME TO PLAY WITH NOUNS AND ACTION VERBS

Another game to play with action verbs *and* nouns, is to write a few sentences and then take out some of the nouns and action verbs. Put blank lines where those words were, then have a friend fill in the blank lines. Like this:

The cat tried to chase the dog all day long.

People didn't understand why the cat was acting this way.

But then a mouse started chasing the cat!

This made everybody jump up and down and laugh a long time.

Now let's take out some of the nouns and action verbs.

The _____ tried to _____ the _____ all day long.
     noun   *action verb*   *noun*

_____ didn't _____ why the _____ was acting this way.
noun   *action verb*   *noun*

But then a _____ started chasing the _____!
           noun   *noun*

This made everybody _____ up and down and ____ a long time.
                      action verb   *action verb*

You can even find books full of these fill-in-the-word games. They're a lot of fun to play with friends or family.

Verbs that show action help make your writing interesting and fun to read.

WHAT IS A VERB?

VERBS THAT SHOW BEING

Remember that verbs are words that tell what a person or thing does or the way it is. Verbs that tell what a person or thing does are action verbs. Some verbs don't show action. They show that something exists or the way it exists.

For example:

He is here.

I am happy.

They are friends.

WHAT IS A VERB?

Verbs that show that something exists or the way it exists are called **being verbs**.

Here are some more examples:

Who <u>was</u> here?

I <u>am</u> tall.

You <u>were</u> younger then.

It <u>is</u> a new bicycle.

21

WHAT IS A VERB?

She *is* over there.

She *is* hungry.

I *am* happy.

22

WHAT IS A VERB?

We talked about how there are many, many action verbs. For being verbs, there aren't very many. There are others, but these are the most common being verbs:

be
being
is
am
are
was
were

Being verbs may not be as exciting as action verbs, but sometimes you need them in your writing to say that something exists or to say the way it exists.

VERBS CAN WORK TOGETHER

Sometimes verbs have helping words.

These helping words are also verbs. They work with the action verb or being verb.

Here are some examples. Can you tell which is the helping verb and which is the main verb?

*She **is** talking to her brother.*

WHAT IS A VERB?

The dog **can** eat.

He **might** like the treat.

You **should** look more closely.

WHAT IS A VERB?

The helping verbs in these sentences are the ones in darker color. The main verbs are the ones next to them that are also underlined.

Can you spot the helping verbs in these sentences?

*The boy **does** <u>eat</u> quickly.*

*The turtle **will** <u>like</u> the warm bath.*

*The giraffe **can** <u>reach</u> very high.*

All the examples so far were helping verbs with action verbs.

Let's try some examples where helping verbs are working together with being verbs.

*The night **will** <u>be</u> cold.*

WHAT IS A VERB?

*They **are** being quiet.*

Let's see how helping verbs change sentences to make them mean something different:

Just a main verb	With a helping verb
Jet airplanes fly very high.	*Jet airplanes **are** flying very high.*
A cat is here.	*A cat **has** been here.*
The paint spilled everywhere!	*The paint **is** spilling everywhere!*
We are quiet.	*We **should** be quiet.*
Jayden feels happy on his birthday.	*Jayden **will** feel happy on his birthday.*
Sal loves math.	*Sal **might** love math.*
Teresa came over.	*Teresa **is** coming over.*

WHAT IS A VERB?

Wow! We have talked a lot about verbs! You probably are starting to feel like an expert on the subject of verbs!

Not so fast—there are still more fun things to learn about verbs.

Just turn ... the... page...↪

Noun or Verb?

One of the fun things about words is that certain words can be either a noun or a verb.

It's just like people. You can be a student sometimes and a friend other times. It depends on what you are doing.

Words are the same. It depends on what they are doing.

For example, the word *brush* can be a noun or a verb.

I have a new brush.

Or

In the morning, I brush my hair.

NOUN OR VERB?

Which one is a noun and which one is a verb?

(The first one is a noun because it names a thing. The second is a verb that shows action.)

Here's another example, this time using the word *box*:

That's a big box!

My brother likes to box with his friends.

Can you tell which is the noun and which is the verb?

(The first one is a noun, the second one is a verb.)

Now, try this one with the word *trip*, which might be a little harder. (Remember that a noun is a word that names a person, place or thing, but you can't always touch it. A verb is a word showing action or being.)

My family took a trip last summer.

Someone might trip on that piece of wood.

Which *trip* is a noun and which is a verb?

NOUN OR VERB?

(You might think the first one is a verb because taking a trip shows an action, but the word *trip* is naming a thing that happened. The word *trip* in the second sentence is a verb because it shows an action.)

Here's one that might be easier, this time with the word *swim*:

We went for a swim.

When I swim, I feel like a dolphin.

Can you see the difference? (The first one is a noun, the second one is a verb.)

There are actually many words that can be nouns or verbs. It all depends on the job it is doing in the sentence. Can you think of any others? (Hint: If you look in a dictionary that shows what words are nouns and what words are verbs, you might be able to find some that are both.)

It's kind of fun seeing how some words can be nouns sometimes and verbs other times.

Knowing the difference can help you use the right word in the right way, which helps you write sentences that people love to read!

Past, Present or Future?

One of the things that sentences tell us is when something happens.

Let's look at these three sentences that are almost the same:

Josef kicks the soccer ball toward the goal.

Josef will kick the soccer ball toward the goal.

Josef kicked the soccer ball toward the goal.

Did you see the differences?

The first one shows that it's happening now.

Josef kicks the soccer ball toward the goal.

The second sentence says that it will happen in the future.

Josef will kick the soccer ball toward the goal.

And the third one shows that it happened in the past.

Josef kicked the soccer ball toward the goal.

What kind of word is *kick*? It shows an action, right? It's an action verb!

PAST, PRESENT OR FUTURE?

Verbs can show action or being, but they also tell when things are happening!

These three sentences show you how you can change a verb to make it show when something is happening—in the present (now), in the future, or in the past.

The different names for verbs that tell when something is happening are

present tense   *past tense*   *future tense*

Usually, the word tense means when you feel nervous and not very relaxed, like this:

My sister told me I was too <u>tense</u> and that I should relax about things.

But when you are talking about verbs, **tense** means the time you are talking about.

Present tense means the time that is happening in the present, right now. **Future tense** means time in the future. **Past tense** means time in the past.

Let's go over each verb tense, one at a time.

PAST, PRESENT OR FUTURE?

PRESENT TENSE

The present is now. Verbs that talk about something that is happening now are **present tense** verbs.

Today the girl jumps rope.

He sings very loudly.

I am ten years old.

FUTURE TENSE

Verbs that talk about something that will happen in the future are **future tense.** This tense is made by adding the helping verb *will* to the verb.

We will play our best in the next game.

Next year, the girl will learn to dance.

I will visit my grandparents.

PAST, PRESENT OR FUTURE?

PAST TENSE

Verbs that talk about things that already happened are **past tense** verbs.

Tuesday

Wednesday

I baked the cake yesterday.

I ran to my friend's house last week.

The boy was nine years old last month.

Knowing about the different verb tenses helps you write more clearly because people will know when the things happened that you are writing about!

Funny Verbs

When you change the tense of a verb, it's usually very easy. But sometimes weird, unusual things happen. That's why this chapter is called "Funny Verbs." The word **funny** can mean something that makes you laugh, but it also can mean something weird or unusual. For example, in France people often kiss each other on both cheeks when they say hello. To Americans, that can seem like a *funny* way to say hello because it seems unusual.

Some verbs are a little unusual, especially in the past tense. People who are learning English might think they're weird or *funny*.

But first let's talk about the present tense.

PRESENT TENSE

Present tense verbs have two different forms, the normal form and one that adds an *s*. And this is something you already know, even though you don't think about it.

FUNNY VERBS

Here's an example:

I walk home. *The family walks home.*

You walk home. *She walks home.*

We walk home. *The boy walks home.*

They walk home. *The animal walks home.*

A young child might say, "It walk home!" But eventually the child will learn to say, "It walks home!" because they learn that it sounds better.

Maybe you've heard people just learning English say something like, "She walk home." But when they learn English better, they will learn to say it correctly: "She walks home."

If you choose some other verbs and use them with different persons or things, you will see how it almost always works this way. Try some other present tense verbs like *run, skip* or *jog* in place of *walk* and *walks* in the sentences we just looked at. You'll see that the *s* is always added in the same places.

FUNNY VERBS

Sometimes instead of adding an *s* you have to add *es*. Try these words in the above sentences in place of *walk*: *rush*, *dash* or *march*. *Rush* becomes *rushes*. *Dash* becomes *dashes*. *March* becomes *marches*.

Adding *s* or *es* is the usual way to make present tense verbs.

There's one verb that is unusual in the present tense. It's the verb *be*. Let's look at the different present tense forms of *be*.

We are happy.

The animal is happy.

I am happy.

You are happy.

They are happy.

She is happy.

He is happy.

If you said, "I be happy," or "She be happy," that doesn't sound right! You just know that "I am happy" and "She is happy" sound right!

FUNNY VERBS

When something is **regular**, it is done in the usual way. When something is **irregular**, that means it is unusual. It is not done in the usual way.

The verb *be* is irregular because it's unusual. You don't make the different form just by adding an *s* like you do with all the other present tense verbs.

All languages have certain funny things about their grammar. In English, one of the funny things about grammar is irregular verbs.

In the present tense, *be* is the funny one. But in the past tense, there are many irregular verbs!

PAST TENSE

How do you usually turn a verb into the past tense?

Present tense *walk* turns into past tense *walked*, right? What about *talk*, *jump* or *smell*? They are the same. You just add *ed* and it turns into past tense!

If the verb already ends in *e*, you don't need to add *ed* but just a *d*. For example, *stumble*, *hope* and *live* turn into *stumbled*, *hoped* and *lived*.

These words that only need a *d* or *ed* to make the past tense are regular verbs. Here are some examples.

Present	Past
I dance	*I danced*
We visit	*We visited*
They jump	*They jumped*
I laugh	*I laughed*

My sister and I walked to the park yesterday.

My family lived in Canada last year.

We visited so many amazing places during our summer vacation.

So, what about the funny ones? What about the irregular past tense verbs?

Remember how present tense only had one irregular verb, *be*?

Past tense has many irregular verbs!

What would the past tense be for these verbs?

FUNNY VERBS

Present Tense

I run fast today.

John sings a song today.

I see sunshine today.

She wears nice clothes today.

Past Tense

I _____ fast yesterday.

John _____ a song yesterday.

I _____ sunshine yesterday.

She _____ nice clothes yesterday.

If you said *ran*, *sang*, *saw* and *wore*, you were right! If they were regular, they would be *runned*, *sanged*, *seed* and *weared*!

Now you see why we called them funny verbs! They don't make the past tense in the regular way.

They are irregular verbs!

Here are some examples of irregular verbs:

Present Tense	Past Tense
I fly	I flew
I see	I saw
we think	we thought
I wear	I wore
they sleep	they slept
I write	I wrote
I sing	I sang
I bite	I bit
he drinks	he drank
she eats	she ate

And remember how *be* was irregular in present tense? Guess what! It's irregular in past tense also!

Present Tense	Past Tense
I am happy.	*I was happy.*
You are happy.	*You were happy.*
We are happy.	*We were happy.*
She is happy.	*She was happy.*

The past tense of *be* is either *was* or *were* depending on who or what it is.

FUTURE TENSE

If you were wondering what the funny verbs are in future tense, you may be disappointed.

THERE AREN'T ANY!

To make the future tense of any verb, just add the word *will*!

Here are a few examples of all three tenses for a few words:

Present Tense	Past Tense	Future Tense
I laugh	*I laughed*	*I will laugh*
He sings	*He sang*	*He will sing*
Hetty plays	*Hetty played*	*Hetty will play*
I study	*I studied*	*I will study*
Marco swims	*Marco swam*	*Marco will swim*

FUNNY VERBS

And here is how our favorite irregular verb *be* changes in the different tenses.

Present Tense	Past Tense	Future Tense
I am	*I was*	*I will be*
you are	*you were*	*you will be*
he is	*he was*	*he will be*
we are	*we were*	*we will be*
they are	*they were*	*they will be*

Ok, now you really are becoming an expert on verbs!

You know about action verbs like *run*.

You know about being verbs like *is*.

You know that sometimes the same word can be a verb or noun, depending on how it's used.

You know about present tense, past tense and future tense.

And you know about those funny verbs called *irregular verbs*.

GUESS WHAT?

There's more!

ing?

Here's the last neat thing about verbs, and it's very simple. You already use this kind of verb in your speaking and writing all the time!

When you want to say that an action is continuing, you add the letters "ing" to the end of the word.

Action	Continuing Action
run	*running*
play	*playing*
dream	*dreaming*
think	*thinking*
live	*living*

ING?

If it's continuing in the present, you use *is* or *are* or *am* with the verb and put *ing* on the end of the verb.

Action	Continuing Action
He sings.	*He is singing.*
She talks.	*She is talking.*
They walk.	*They are walking.*
I feel better.	*I am feeling better.*
He swims well.	*He is swimming well.*

Did you see how the sentences on the left were a little bit different than the sentences on the right? The ones on the right say that the action is continuing.

You can also show that an action was continuing in the past. Use *was* or *were* with the verb and put *ing* on the end of the verb.

Past Action	Continuing Action in the Past
I bowled.	*I was bowling.*
You looked at me.	*You were looking at me.*
They sang all day.	*They were singing all day.*
We held our breath.	*We were holding our breath.*

To show an action continuing in the future, just add *will be* and *ing*.

Future Action	Continuing Action in the Future
I will write.	I will be writing.
We will sing.	We will be singing.
They will walk.	They will be walking.
She will feel happy.	She will be feeling happy.

See how easy it is to show that an action is continuing!

If you listen to people talking, or listen to yourself, or pick up the book you are reading, or even look at your own stories, you will probably find that everybody uses these *ing* verbs a lot.

Try it!

And now you really are an expert on verbs!

Words that Describe 9

One of the most fun things about writing sentences is using words to describe things.

Describe means to use words that tell more.

When you use words to describe, the person reading your writing has a better idea of what you are writing about.

If you were describing a dog, for example, you might say what color it is, how big or small it is, whether it's happy or sad, or lonely, or mean, or friendly. You are telling more about the dog, which helps your reader get a better idea of the dog.

You can use describing words with nouns, like the word dog.

dog   *brown dog*

Brown tells you more about the dog.

WORDS THAT DESCRIBE

You can also use describing words with a verb.

running

running *fast*

Fast tells you how the boy is running.

You can even use describing words to tell more about other describing words.

>The boy was running *fast*.

>The boy was running *very fast*.

Here's another example:

>The *brown* dog was *excited*.

>The *dark brown* dog was *super excited*.

Dark tells more about the describing word *brown*. *Super* tells more about the describing word *excited*.

Describing words can make a huge difference when you are trying to write sentences that people will love. Try it for yourself and see what you think!

What Is an Adjective? 10

The first kind of describing word is an **adjective**. It's a word that tells more about nouns, like this:

little girl   *tall* girl

Little and *tall* are adjectives. They tell you more about the noun *girl*.

WHAT IS AN ADJECTIVE?

<u>skinny</u> cat   <u>fat</u> cat

Skinny and *fat* are adjectives. They tell more about the noun *cat*.

The <u>friendly</u> girl wore a <u>cool</u> hat.

Friendly tells more about the noun *girl*. *Cool* tells more about the noun *hat*.

The <u>long</u> snake moved in the <u>green</u> grass.

Long tells more about the noun *snake*. *Green* tells more about the noun *grass*.

By using different adjectives, you can make boring sentences more interesting. Here are some examples:

Kind of boring:

I ate a pineapple.

More interesting:

I ate a <u>delicious</u> pineapple.

Kind of boring:

We have a tree in our yard that I like to climb.

WHAT IS AN ADJECTIVE?

More interesting:

We have a huge tree in our yard that I like to climb.

Kind of boring:

My mom came to get me at the playground.

More interesting:

My angry mom came to get me at the playground.

So far all the adjectives have come right before the noun, like

delicious pineapple

huge tree

angry mom

Sometimes the adjective comes after the noun. Let's look at these examples:

Federica is smart.

The police officer was patient.

That jet is fast!

They tell more about the nouns that came before them.

But most of the time, you will find adjectives right before the nouns they tell more about.

Wherever you put them, you can have a lot of fun using adjectives!

What Is an Adverb?

Words used to describe verbs are called *adverbs*. Here are some examples:

Winnie quickly ran over to my house.

The adverb *quickly* tells how Winnie ran. It tells more about the verb *ran*.

I whispered quietly, telling him to promise not to tell my secret to anyone!

The adverb *quietly* tells more about the verb *whispered*.

Our father happily showed us the new tent.

Can you tell which word *happily* describes? If you said *showed*, you are right! *Showed* is an action verb that is described by the adverb *happily*.

But are you ready for another funny thing about English grammar? Adverbs don't just describe verbs. They also describe adjectives!

Not only that, they also describe other adverbs!

So, an **adverb** is a word that describes verbs, adjectives and other adverbs.

Let's go over each of these. We'll start with the one we already gave a few examples of.

WHAT IS AN ADVERB?

ADVERBS WITH VERBS

An adverb tells more about a verb. It tells *how* the verb happens, *where* it happens or *when* it happens, like this:

how

He is singing.   He is singing loudly.

Loudly is an adverb. It tells you how he is singing.

where

The bird flies.   The bird flies high.

High is an adverb. It tells you where the bird is flying.

WHAT IS AN ADVERB?

when

The boy read.   *The boy read late.*

Late is an adverb. It tells you <u>when</u> the boy read.

Look at each of the following sentences and decide how the adverb is telling more about the verb. Is it saying *how, where* or *when*? (Answers for the first three are given. The rest of the answers are given after all the sentences.)

The wind blew <u>loudly</u>.	(tells *how* the wind blew)
My birthday party happens <u>today</u>.	(tells when my birthday party happens)
My brother ran <u>inside</u>.	(tell where my brother ran)

Now your turn:

She paints <u>beautifully</u>.	(how, where or when?)
The elephant trumpeted <u>loudly</u>.	(how, where or when?)
<u>Today</u> we are all going to church.	(how, where or when?)

WHAT IS AN ADVERB?

They all went <u>out</u>.   (how, where or when?)

Viola <u>quickly</u> forgot.   (how, where or when?)

The turtle walked <u>slowly</u>.   (how, where or when?)

She <u>always</u> talks.   (how, where or when?)

I lost it <u>somewhere</u>.   (how, where or when?)

Malcolm will speak <u>here</u> <u>tomorrow</u>.   (two adverbs, which one says when and which one says where?)

(Answers: *beautifully* tells how, *loudly* tells how, *today* tells when, *out* tells where, *quickly* tells how, *slowly* tells how, *always* tells when, *somewhere* tells where, *here* tells where and *tomorrow* tells when.) How did you do?

When adverbs describe verbs, they always tell *how, where* or *when*. This helps you write better sentences because people have a better idea of what you are describing!

Now let's talk about the next thing adverbs can do.

WHAT IS AN ADVERB?

ADVERBS WITH ADJECTIVES

An adverb can tell more about an adjective.

The sky is blue.

The sky is light blue.

Blue is an adjective that tells you more about the *sky*. *Light* is an adverb that tells you more about *blue*.

Ashanti looks great in her green dress!

Ashanti looks great in her dark green dress!

Green is an adjective that tells more about the dress. *Dark* is an adverb that tells more about *green*.

59

WHAT IS AN ADVERB?

The happy dog knocked me over.

The super happy dog knocked me over.

Happy is an adjective that tells more about the dog. *Super* is an adverb that tells the reader more about how happy the dog was.

Here's one more:

Joshua is hungry.

Joshua is extremely hungry.

Hungry is an adjective that tells more about Joshua. *Extremely* is an adverb that tells more about how hungry Joshua really is.

Let's try some different adverbs in the same sentence. All of them are used to tell more about the adjective *strong*.

Miles is very strong.

Miles is fairly strong.

Miles is particularly strong.

Miles is wonderfully strong.

Miles is slightly strong.

Miles is truly strong.

You can see how adverbs can help you tell more about adjectives!

Now, let's talk about the funny one!

WHAT IS AN ADVERB?

ADVERBS WITH OTHER ADVERBS

An adverb can tell more about another adverb.

It is snowing <u>hard</u>. *It is snowing <u>really</u> <u>hard</u>.*

Hard is an adverb that tells you how it is *snowing*. *Really* tells how *hard*.

He is running <u>fast</u> today. *He is running <u>very</u> <u>fast</u> today.*

Fast is an adverb that tells you *how* he is running. *Very* is an adverb that tells you more about how *fast*.

61

WHAT IS AN ADVERB?

Here are some more examples of an adverb telling more about another adverb.

The storm moved <u>swiftly</u>.	The storm moved <u>very</u> <u>swiftly</u>.
He plays <u>quietly</u>.	He plays <u>awfully</u> <u>quietly</u>.
The cow mooed <u>loudly</u>.	The cow mooed <u>really</u> <u>loudly</u>.
The bird flew <u>up</u>.	The bird flew <u>way</u> <u>up</u>.
Violet <u>quickly</u> remembered.	Violet <u>very</u> <u>quickly</u> remembered.
Joe was speaking <u>slowly</u>.	Joe was speaking <u>so</u> <u>slowly</u>.
She <u>always</u> comes.	She <u>almost</u> <u>always</u> comes.

You can use adjectives and adverbs to make your writing even more interesting.

Take a look at these examples showing how describing words make the sentences so much more interesting.

The eagle flew in circles.	The lonely eagle flew silently in lazy circles.
The balloon rose.	The bright blue balloon rose very quickly.
Li played with the kittens.	Li quietly played with the five fuzzy kittens.

Are you ready for more about words that describe? Keep going!

A, An and The

There are three little words that you use all the time. They are the words this chapter is all about: *a*, *an* and *the*.

Let's start by talking about another funny thing in English. It's about the first two words: *a* and *an*.

Did you ever wonder why you sometimes say *a* and sometimes say *an*?

I ate an apple.   *I ate a banana.*

I ate an orange.   *I ate a pear.*

I ate an almond.   *I ate a marshmallow.*

The sentences on the left all use *an* but the sentences on the right use *a*.

Hm. Why?

Well, one good reason is that it sounds right! It doesn't sound right to say them this way:

I ate a apple.   *I ate an banana.*

I ate a orange.   *I ate an pear.*

I ate a almond.   *I ate an marshmallow.*

A, AN AND THE

But you could use the word *the* in place of those words. Let's try it:

I ate the apple. *I ate the banana.*

I ate the orange. *I ate the pear.*

I ate the almond. *I ate the marshmallow.*

Those all sound right!

A, *an*, and *the* are special adjectives called **articles**. They are used in front of nouns when you want to talk about just one thing.

an apple—that means just one apple

a ball—that means just one ball

the cat—that means just one cat

The difference is that when you write *a* or *an* before a noun, it means you are not saying which one of those things you are talking about.

A dog means any dog. *A marshmallow* means any marshmallow.

An apple means any apple. *An orange* means any orange.

I want a dog.

A doesn't tell which dog. It could be any one of them.

A, AN AND THE

I am going to buy <u>an</u> apple.

An doesn't tell which apple. It could be any one of them.

When *the* comes before a noun, it means you are talking about one certain thing.

When you say *the dog* you are talking about a certain dog.

I want <u>the</u> dog with spots.

When you write *the apple* you are talking about a certain apple.

I am going to buy <u>the</u> apple that is biggest.

A, AN AND THE

So, when you say *a* or *an*, you are just talking about any one. When you say *the*, you are talking about a certain one, not just any one.

But what about that funny thing where sometimes you use *a* and sometimes you use *an*?

The answer is that it depends on how the noun that comes after it sounds!

A comes before nouns that start with a <u>consonant</u> sound.

a <u>b</u>ook

a <u>r</u>oom

a <u>j</u>acket

a <u>l</u>ion

a <u>s</u>tory

An means the same thing as *a,* but it comes before nouns that start with a vowel sound.

an <u>e</u>lephant

an <u>a</u>pple

an <u>o</u>ctopus

But what about a word like *hour*? Do you say *an hour* or do you say *a hour*?

You probably said the right answer. You say *an hour.* But why? The letter *h* is a consonant, not a vowel!

The reason is because the word *hour* starts with a vowel *sound*. Say these sentences and listen for the sound.

The play starts in <u>an</u> hour.

I will work for <u>an</u> hour and then have lunch.

You use *an* because the word *hour* sounds like *our*. The *h* doesn't make any sound.

Now you know all about the words *a, an* and *the*.

They are a special kind of describing word called an *article*. They tell the person reading your writing that you are talking about just one thing.

If it's just any one, you use *a* or *an*.

If it's a certain one, you use *the*.

Simple!

Wow, Look What You Know! 13

You know so much about grammar now, you should be able to write some great sentences.

You know all about how to use *nouns* to name a person, place or thing.

airplane
unicorn
baseball
teacher
pen
shoe
umbrella
computer

You know all about using *action verbs* to show action.

run
play
jump
sing
write
read
talk
laugh

WOW, LOOK WHAT YOU KNOW!

You know all about using *being verbs* to show the way something is.

am
is
are
was
were
be

You know all about how to make *past, present and future tenses* of verbs.

I rode my bike.

I ride my bike.

I will ride my bike.

You even know how to show that an action is continuing by adding a *helping verb* and *ing*!

I <u>am</u> rid<u>ing</u> my bike.

She <u>is</u> talk<u>ing</u> to you.

That tiger <u>is</u> eat<u>ing</u> a big steak!

You know all about how to use *adjectives* to tell more about nouns.

the <u>big</u> dog

the <u>purple</u> car

an <u>exciting</u> story

WOW, LOOK WHAT YOU KNOW!

You know all about how to use *adverbs* to tell more about verbs, adjectives and other adverbs.

That girl runs <u>fast</u>!

She has <u>very</u> strong legs.

But she sure runs <u>super</u> quietly!

And you know all about how to use the *articles a, an* and *the* to say that you are just talking about one thing.

a banana

an octopus

the car

You're a grammar star!

How to Stop a Sentence

Now that you know how to use nouns to name things, verbs to show action, and adjectives and adverbs to describe things, you can start to write some great sentences!

Let's try it.

> *The frightened boy looked through the bars at the huge gorilla he went to the zoo to see gorillas but the big animal made him suddenly very scared right then the gorilla looked straight at the little boy and made a big sound the boy ran away very fast the gorilla wondered where did the boy go*

That's a great sentence, isn't it?

Well, not exactly. It uses lots of nouns and verbs. It uses lots of adjectives, adverbs and articles. But something is wrong with it.

It's too long! It just goes on and on and on!

People don't love to read sentences that never stop. And that's what this chapter is about: how to stop a sentence!

HOW TO STOP A SENTENCE

That brings us to a new word: punctuation (PUNG-chew-AY-shun).

Punctuation is when you use certain marks in writing to tell the reader when to slow down or stop or how to read the sentence.

Do you know what marks you can use to end a sentence?

Let's try to fix the writing about the boy and the gorilla using marks to end every sentence.

> The frightened boy looked through the bars at the huge gorilla. He went to the zoo to see gorillas but the big animal made him suddenly very scared! Right then the gorilla looked straight at the little boy and made a big sound. The boy ran away very fast! The gorilla wondered where did the boy go?

Now you can tell when to slow down or stop. You can also tell that some sentences are supposed to be exciting and one of them is a question. How?

When you write, there are three punctuation marks you can use to show the end of a sentence.

These are

1. the period **.**
2. the question mark **?**
3. the exclamation point **!**

A **period** goes at the end of a sentence that tells something.

> The bus went down the road.
>
> Birds are my favorite animals.

HOW TO STOP A SENTENCE

A **question mark** goes at the end of a sentence that asks something.

> *Where are you going?*
>
> *Is your hair red?*

An **exclamation point** goes at the end of a sentence that shows strong feeling or surprise. If you're very happy or very angry, you can use an exclamation point.

> *I love it!*
>
> *What a great shot!*
>
> *Wow, it's an alligator!*
>
> *I hate you, Robert!*

Oh, one more thing. Sometimes people call the *exclamation point* an *exclamation mark*. They mean the same thing. It's just two different names for it!

Every sentence has one of these three punctuation marks at the end. That's how you know the sentence is done.

Let's look at the boy and gorilla story again.

> *The frightened boy looked through the bars at the huge gorilla. He went to the zoo to see gorillas but the big animal made him suddenly very scared! Right then the gorilla looked straight at the little boy and made a big sound. The boy ran away very fast! The gorilla wondered where did the boy go?*

How many sentences does the story have?

HOW TO STOP A SENTENCE

That's right. Five. Two of them end with a period. Two of them end with an exclamation point. And the last one ends with a question mark.

To write sentences that people love to read, you need to know how to use these punctuation marks. Otherwise, your sentences will just go on and on and on and on and on and on and on and on and on ....

How to Pause a Sentence 15

You know how to get someone to stop at the end of a sentence. You use one of the punctuation marks we learned in the last chapter.

But what if you don't want them to stop, but you just want them to pause.

A **comma** is a punctuation mark that looks like this **,**

It tells the reader where to take a pause when they are reading.

Expert writers know lots of different rules for when to use commas. Sometimes they even disagree on the rules!

But for now, let's talk about just two ways you can use commas to write sentences that people will love:

1. A comma is used to separate items on a list.

   I need to buy eggs, bread and chocolate.

   In my garden I planted flowers, green beans, tomatoes and corn.

   My sister likes to eat apples, peanut butter, raisins and cookies.

HOW TO PAUSE A SENTENCE

2. A comma is used at the beginning and end of a letter or message to someone, like this:

Dear Sasha,

I am excited to see you this summer. Be sure to bring your skateboard when you come so we can ride together.

See you soon,

Hank

Simple, isn't it?

Yes, there are other rules for commas and you can try to use them in your writing if you want to. The main rule for using a comma is that you use it when you want the reader to pause, but not STOP.

You now have four punctuation marks you can use to write sentences people love to read.

Do you remember what all four of them are called?

? . ! ,

How to Start Sentences and Names

16

You know how to stop a sentence, but do you know how to start one?

You can start a sentence almost any way you want, but there's one thing you always do.

STARTING A SENTENCE

The first word in a sentence always starts with a capital letter.

The dog bit the boy.

Turtles move slowly.

This helps the person reading your sentence be sure it's a new sentence.

You probably already knew that rule.

Did you know there are more rules about using capital letters?

HOW TO START SENTENCES AND NAMES

NAMING PEOPLE AND THINGS

The names of people, pets, schools, cities, special groups and places all start with capital letters.

Sarah   Amazon River

Thumper   Himalayan Mountains

Oak Crest Private School   California

Boston   United States

London   New England Patriots (a football team)

DAYS OF THE WEEK

The names of the days of the week start with capital letters.

Sunday   Tuesday   Thursday   Saturday

Monday   Wednesday   Friday

NAMES OF THE MONTHS

The names of the months start with capital letters.

January   April   July   October

February   May   August   November

March   June   September   December

HOW TO START SENTENCES AND NAMES

BUT NOT THE SEASONS

The names of the seasons do *not* start with capital letters.

summer   *fall*   *winter*   *spring*

That's just another one of those funny rules in English! You capitalize the days of the week and the months of the year, but you don't capitalize the seasons.

How to Write a Great Sentence

17

Do you remember early in the book how we described what a sentence is?

A **sentence** is a whole idea put into words so that it makes sense.

The idea can be short or long, funny, serious, simple, excited or curious. No matter what kind of sentence it is, you can make it a great one if you know how sentences work.

PARTS OF A SENTENCE

A sentence usually has three parts:

1. *A noun that tells what the sentence is about.*

2. *A verb that tells what the noun is doing or the way it is.*

3. *Other words that usually tell more about the noun and verb.*

HOW TO WRITE A GREAT SENTENCE

The noun a sentence is about is called the **subject** of the sentence.

The boy is kicking the ball.
  subject

The house is blue.
  subject

HOW TO WRITE A GREAT SENTENCE

The <u>axe</u> hit the log.
subject

The <u>jet</u> zooms across the sky.
subject

Even a very simple sentence has a subject.

<u>Jade</u> plays.
subject

HOW TO WRITE A GREAT SENTENCE

The second part of every sentence is the verb that tells what the subject is doing.

The boy is kicking the ball.
         verb

The house is blue.
         verb

The axe hit the log.
         verb

The jet zooms across the sky.
         verb

Even the very simple sentence has a verb.

Jade plays.
     verb

Every sentence has at least a subject and a verb.

Here are some examples with the subjects marked in red and the verbs in blue:

We walked home yesterday.

Bettina kissed her father gently on the cheek.

Rodrigo ate the whole pie!

I can remember when I was two years old.

The leopard chased the swift antelope.

Clouds make me sad.

My grandmother is swimming across the calm lake.

Other words, like adjectives, adverbs and articles, usually tell more about the subject and verb. You might be able to spot some of the adjectives, adverbs and articles in the sentences above.

If you have a subject and a verb, and then you add other words like adjectives, adverbs and articles, you can make great sentences.

But there's more!

SENTENCES THAT TELL

Most sentences tell something. In sentences that tell something, the subject usually comes before the verb. These kinds of sentences are the ones that end in a period or an exclamation point.

I am going to the store.

The pitcher threw the ball.

Melvyn climbs trees every weekend.

Look, those guys are racing up the tree after Melvyn!

But there's another kind of sentence that you also use a lot.

HOW TO WRITE A GREAT SENTENCE

SENTENCES THAT ASK

Sometimes a sentence isn't telling something, it's asking something. This kind of sentence is called a **question**. It's the kind of sentence that ends with a question mark.

In a question, the subject usually comes after the verb.

Where is the ball?

Why are you sad?

How tall is the tree?

What color is your shirt?

Sometimes the subject sits right in between a helping verb and an action verb, like these:

Can Sally laugh?

Are we going now?

Do you like coconut?

Is DeShawn getting a new car?

Can you tell which words are the helping verbs and which ones are the action verbs?

(The helping verbs are Can, Are, Do and Is. The action verbs are laugh, going, like and getting.)

TOO SHORT?

A group of words that doesn't tell a whole idea is an incomplete sentence.

Here are some incomplete sentences with subjects but no verb to tell what's happening.

The morning

The two girls

In December, the weather

Here are some incomplete sentences with verbs but no subjects to go with them.

was cold

went swimming

rains every afternoon

If you write a short sentence and it doesn't sound right, check to make sure you didn't forget the subject or the verb!

HOW TO WRITE A GREAT SENTENCE

TOO LONG?

Sometimes a writer will start a sentence, then write and write without stopping. This makes a sentence that's hard for a reader to understand.

Take a look at this sentence:

> *Summer is my favorite time of year when the weather is warm we can go swimming I can also go to horse camp and soccer camp.*

It has a lot of thoughts all put together. It's pretty hard to figure out what the writer is saying.

Let's break that sentence up with some punctuation.

> *Summer is my favorite time of year. When the weather is warm, we can go swimming. I can also go to horse camp and soccer camp.*

That's better! That has three sentences that all make sense.

There's even a funny name for sentences that just seem to go on and on like they are running and won't stop.

People call a sentence like that a **run-on** sentence! It's a good name, don't you think?

SENTENCES PEOPLE LOVE TO READ

Now you know how to write a great sentence.

It will have a subject and a verb, for sure. And it will probably have some other words that tell more about the subject and the verb.

It won't be too short.

It won't be a run-on sentence.

It might tell or it might ask, but the reader will know because you used the right punctuation mark.

It will start with a capital letter.

It will tell a whole idea and it will make sense!

And the last most important thing about a great sentence is this:

It will say what YOU want it to say!

The Magic Secret   18

In this book you have learned many things.

You learned about grammar, like nouns and verbs, adjectives and adverbs. You even learned about *a, an* and *the*. Do you remember what they're called?

You learned about different kinds of sentences, ones that tell and ones that ask.

You learned different ways to stop a sentence and even how to make the reader pause. Remember? (It's called a comma.)

Hopefully, you have practiced all these things while going through the book. If you did, you are probably pretty good at all of it by now.

But there's one more thing that's even more important than ANYTHING this book has talked about. It's the magic secret about writing sentences that people love to read. In fact, all your most favorite books were written by authors who knew this magic secret.

You might even be able to guess what the secret is. If you want to try to guess, don't turn the page till you are ready.

Okay. Ready?

THE MAGIC SECRET

Write lots of sentences!

And then write more.

And more.

And more.

And more.

And more.

And more.

Now, maybe you had a different idea for what the secret was. Well, your guess might be secret #1 for you! Every great writer has their own secrets for writing great sentences.

But every great writer also knows the secret above or they wouldn't be able to write sentences that people love to read!

You can do it!

Good luck!

And have fun writing!

www.ingramcontent.com/pod-product-compliance
Lightning Source LLC
Chambersburg PA
CBHW080442170426
43195CB00017B/2866